A Children's Book About

SNOOPING

Grolier Enterprises, Inc. offers a varied selection of children's
book racks and tote bags. For details on ordering, please write:
Grolier Enterprises Inc., Sherman Turnpike, Danbury, CT 06816
Attn: Premium Department

Managing Editor: Ellen Klarberg
Copy Editor: Annette Gooch
Editorial Assistant: Lana Eberhard
Art Director: Jennifer Wiezel
Production Artist: Gail Miller
Illustration Designer: Bartholomew
Inking Artist: Barbara Baird
Coloring Artist: Barbara Baird
Lettering Artist: Linda Hanney
Typographer: Communication Graphics

A Children's Book About

SNOOPING

By Joy Berry

GROLIER ENTERPRISES CORP.

This book is about Sam and his sister Maggie.

Reading about Sam and Maggie can help you understand and deal with **snooping.**

You are snooping when you secretly look through other people's things.

You are snooping when you secretly try to find out things about other people.

Snooping is being nosy in a sneaky, meddlesome way.

No one likes it when someone snoops.

It is important to treat others the way you want to be treated.

If you do not want others to snoop, you must not snoop.

It is important to *respect other people.* Do not secretly listen in when others are talking together.

Do not secretly listen in when someone is talking on the telephone.

Do not watch other people without their knowing it.

Do not pry into another person's business.
Do not try to learn things about others that
they might not want you to know.

It is important to *respect other people's property.* Do not look in the windows or doors of people's houses without their knowing it.

Do not go into other people's homes unless you have permission. Do not go into a room in another person's home unless you have permission.

If a door is closed, knock on it and wait to be invited before you go in.

Do not look through another person's dresser drawers, cupboards, or closets unless you have permission.

Do not read things that belong to another person unless you have permission.

It is important *to respect other people's privacy.* People might have some thoughts and feelings they want to keep to themselves.

Do not try to make people share the thoughts and feelings they do not want to share.

If you snoop, others might feel they cannot depend on you. They might feel they cannot trust you.

Snooping can be harmful to you and others. It is not good for you or for the people around you.

It is important to treat other people the way you want to be treated.

If you do not want other people to snoop, you must not snoop.